AMAZING RECORDS
by Kana Riley

Celebration Press

Parsippany, New Jersey

TABLE OF CONTENTS

Fastest, Slowest

Biggest, Smallest

I magine how exciting an Animal Olympics would be! Some vultures can fly as high as jet planes. Some whales can hold their breath and dive nearly a mile underwater. Little ants can lift 50 times their own weight. If you could do that, you could lift a truck over your head!

Animals can be amazing. In fact, all the animals in this book are record-breakers!

Fastest, Slowest
Cheetah

The cheetah is the fastest animal on land. It can run at more than 60 miles per hour. That's the speed a car travels on a highway.

At full speed, each stride of a cheetah covers over 20 feet. If you don't think that's a lot, mark off 20 feet with a measuring tape.

Cheetahs are sprinters—really fast runners. They can only run at top speed for about 300 yards before they begin to slow down. That's usually long enough to catch whatever they are chasing, though!

Swift

A small bird called a swift would win a race with a cheetah. It is the world's fastest flier. The swift's strong wings carry it at speeds up to 100 miles per hour. No wonder they call this bird a swift. *Swift* means fast.

A swift may fly all day. As it flies, it snatches insects out of the air and eats them. Then at night it returns to its nest on a cliff, in a hollow tree, or in a chimney. One small swift may fly up to 135,000 miles in a year.

Peregrine Falcon

A peregrine falcon can move even faster than a swift. The bird circles high above a meadow. Its sharp eyes search for small animals far below. Suddenly it spots one. The peregrine dives, speeding toward the ground at 200 miles per hour. It snatches up its prey and carries it to its nest in a rocky cliff.

In recent years, peregrine falcons have started moving into cities. There they build their nests on tall buildings and bridges instead of cliffs.

Sailfish

The sailfish is not as fast as a falcon. But it is one of the fastest fish. It has big fins, a strong tail, and a streamlined shape. They help the sailfish reach speeds of 68 miles per hour. Like the cheetah, the sailfish can only move at top speed for short distances.

A full-grown sailfish can be about ten feet long. That's almost as long as a small car. The heaviest sailfish ever caught weighed over 200 pounds. That's about as heavy as a refrigerator. What a catch that must have been!

Snail

The snail is the slowpoke of the animal world, creeping along under its shell on one big foot.

Snails move so slowly that it's silly to measure their speed in miles per hour. Look at it this way. A child can walk three miles in an hour. It would take a snail 100 hours to move that far. That's more than four days!

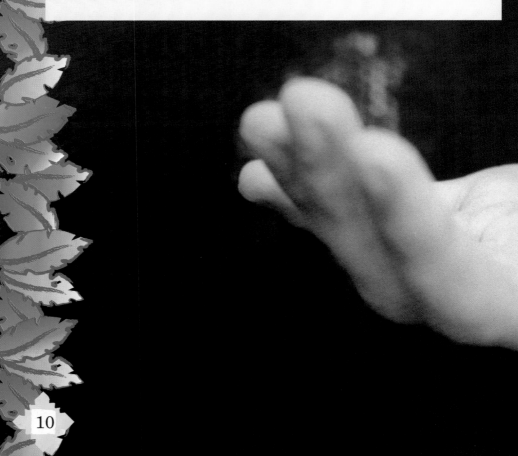

Racing the Animals

Snail	$\frac{3}{100}$ miles per hour
Child walking	3 miles per hour
Man sprinting	22 miles per hour
Cheetah	60 miles per hour
Sailfish	68 miles per hour
Swift	100 miles per hour

0   50   100

How might a person do in a race with these animals? Just look at the graph.

Biggest, Smallest
Elephant

Guess how much an elephant eats.

One African elephant eats 500 pounds of grass, leaves, and fruit every day. So it's not surprising that African elephants are the heaviest animals on land.

A large male elephant can weigh five and a half tons. That's about as much as five medium-sized cars. One of his ears can weigh more than you do—110 pounds!

Elephants may be the heaviest, but they're not the tallest animals.

Giraffe

The giraffe's long neck makes it the tallest of all the animals. Giraffes are 19 feet tall. If your bedroom window were on the second floor of your house, an adult giraffe could look right in your window!

At that height, the giraffe can usually find all the food it wants. It munches on tree leaves no other animals can reach.

Surprisingly, that long giraffe neck has the same number of neck bones as yours—seven.

Sun Jellyfish

The longest animal on earth is the sun jellyfish—an animal with no bones at all. Its tentacles can stretch for 200 feet. If they were stretched out straight in all directions, they could cover an underwater football field!

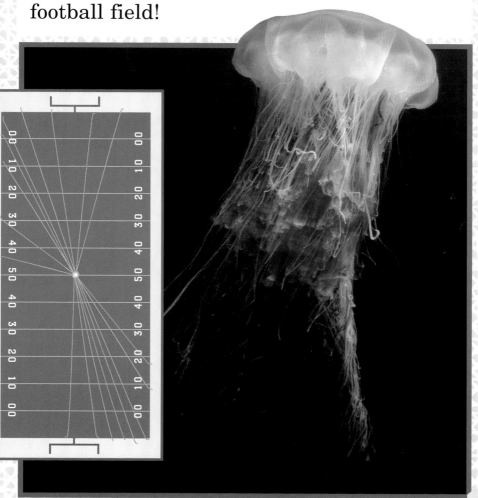

Blue Whale

It weighs 150 tons—25 times what an elephant weighs! It can grow to be 110 feet long—longer than the biggest dinosaur that ever lived! It is a blue whale.

A blue whale baby grows at a rate of 200 pounds per day!

A creature this size could not survive on land. Its huge weight needs the support of the surrounding ocean.

Blue whales are not only big, they are noisy. They make the loudest sound of any animal—louder than a jet engine.

Bee Hummingbird

Here's something a little smaller. The bee hummingbird of Cuba is the smallest bird ever found. It is about three inches long from the tip of its bill to the end of its tail. Its body is only an inch long. It weighs much less than an ounce. In fact, it takes 28 bee hummingbirds to equal the weight of one golf ball.

Like all hummingbirds, this one can fly backward!

Etruscan Shrew

The Etruscan shrew is the world's smallest mammal. Fully grown, it weighs less than a penny (and about the same as the bee hummingbird).

The shrew may be small, but it has a big appetite. Every day it eats three times its weight in insects and worms. Unless it eats every hour or two, it will starve to death.

Animals can be surprisingly fast, tall, big, or small. They can do all kinds of things that people can't. We look at them and say, "Wow! That's amazing!"

The animals don't know they're amazing, though. They're not trying to set Olympic records. They're just doing what comes naturally.

Here's another look at the animal record-breakers.

Fastest land animal	Cheetah	more than 60 miles per hour
Fastest flier	Swift	100 miles per hour
Fastest swimmer	Sailfish	68 miles per hour
Fastest diver	Peregrine Falcon	200 miles per hour
Slowest land animal	Snail	$\frac{3}{100}$ miles per hour
Heaviest land animal	Elephant	$5\frac{1}{2}$ tons
Tallest land animal	Giraffe	more than 19 feet
Longest animal	Sun Jellyfish	up to 200 feet
Largest animal	Blue Whale	150 tons
Smallest bird	Bee Hummingbird	$\frac{6}{100}$ ounce
Smallest mammal	Etruscan Shrew	$\frac{5}{100}$ ounce